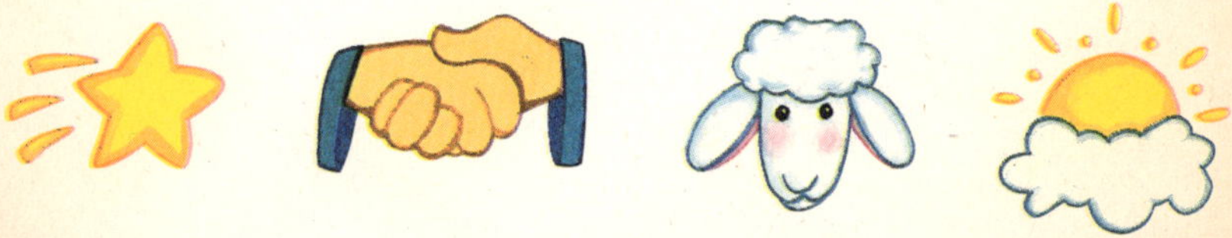

©1995 Landoll, Inc.
Ashland, Ohio 44805
® Little Landoll Books is a trademark owned by Landoll, Inc.
and is registered with the U.S. Patent and Trademark Office.
No part of this book may be reproduced or copied.
All rights reserved. Manufactured in the U.S.A.

GOD
MADE THE WORLD

Written by Dandi

Before the beginning,
There was no blue sky.
No plants and no people,
And nothing to buy!

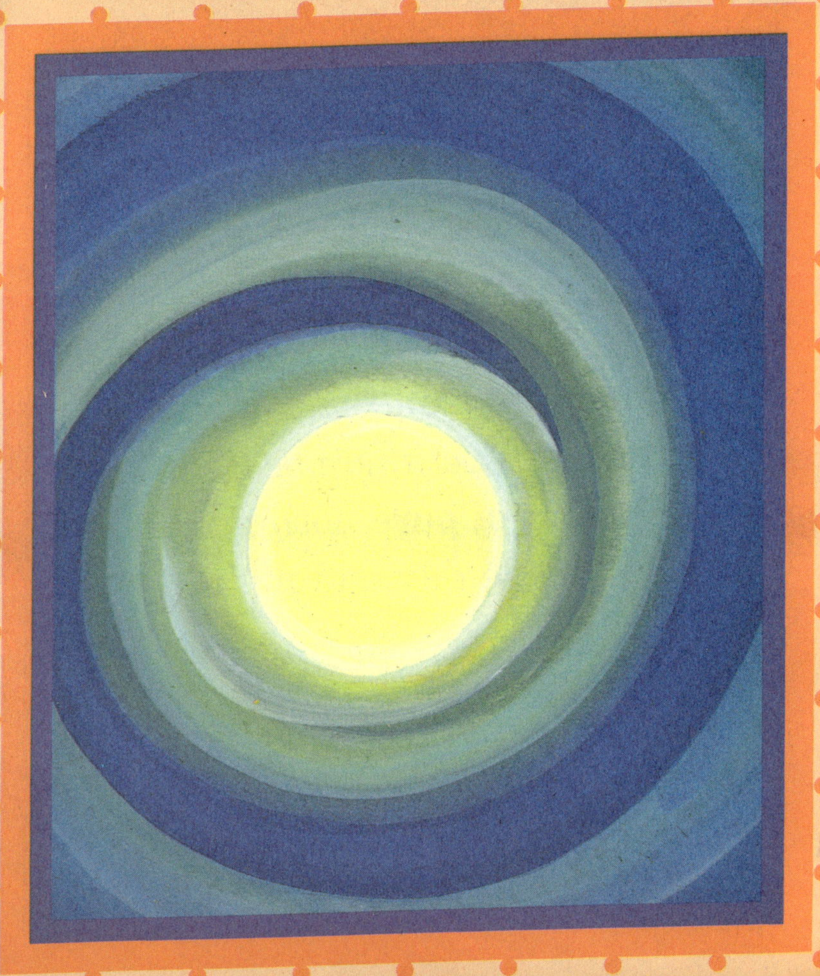

Then God said the word.
He said, *"Let there be light!"*
And out of pure nothing,
God made day and night!

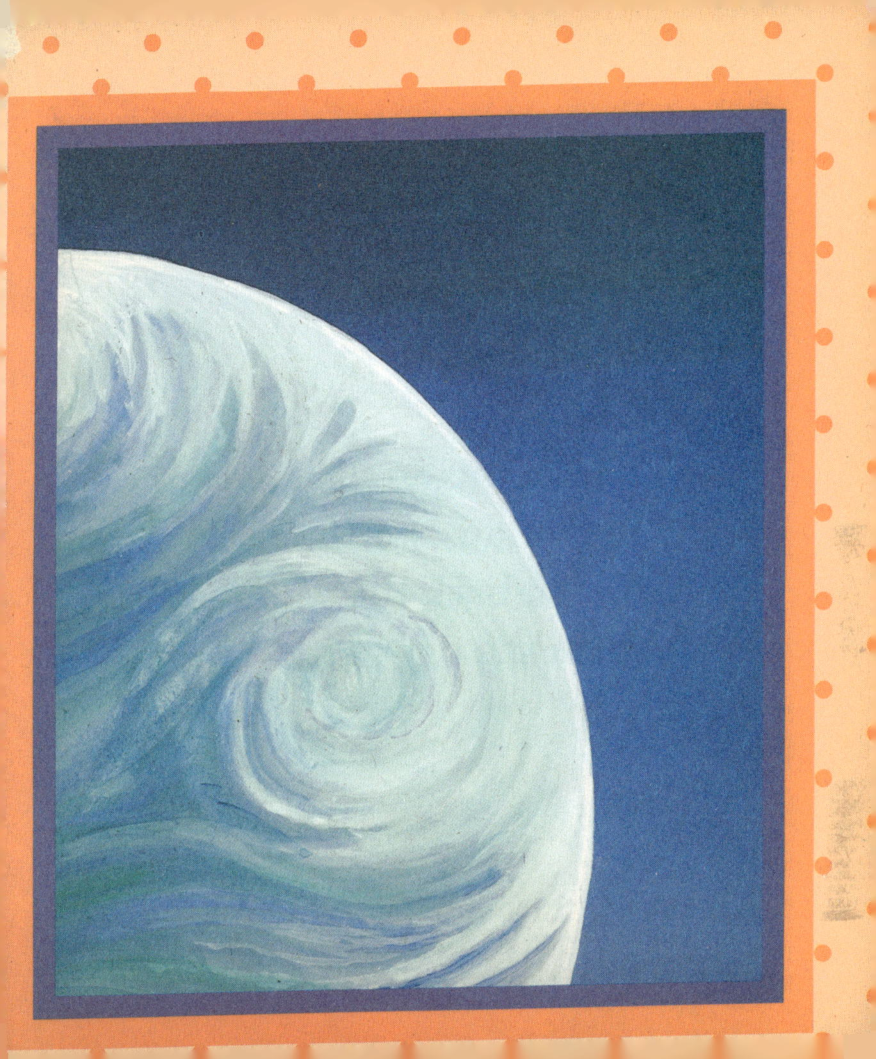

Next, God made the heavens
Of marvelous worth.
And held back the waters
To form the dry earth.

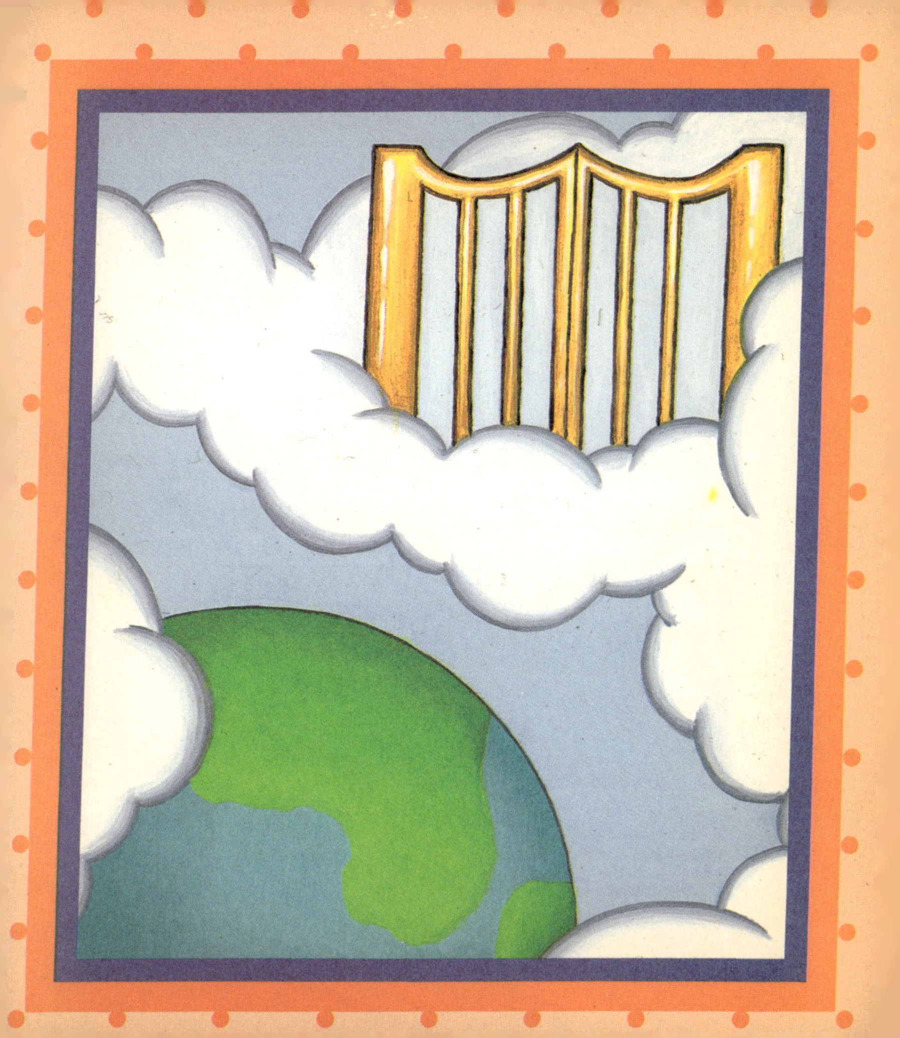

God saw what He did
And said, *"That's pretty good."*
Then followed with flowers
As only God could.

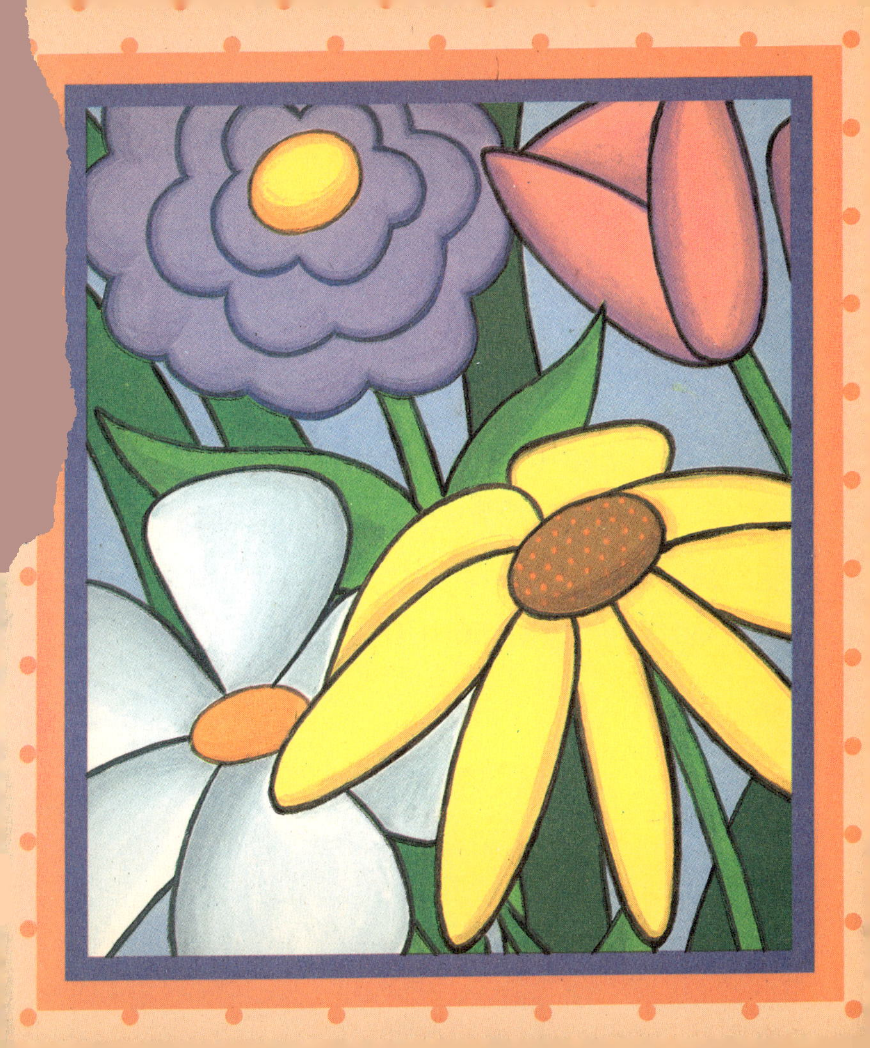

*"We're going to need seasons,
And so just for fun,
I'll whip up a moon
And then throw in a sun."*

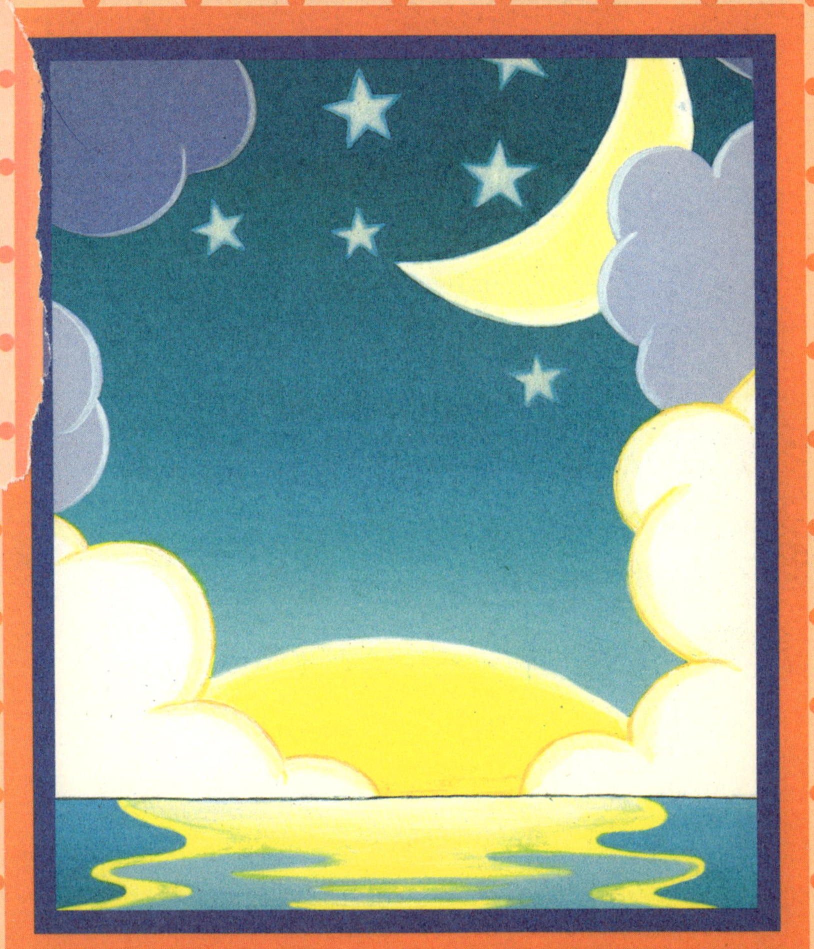

Then next came a robin,
A finch, a bluebird,
And beautiful peacocks,
When God gave the word.

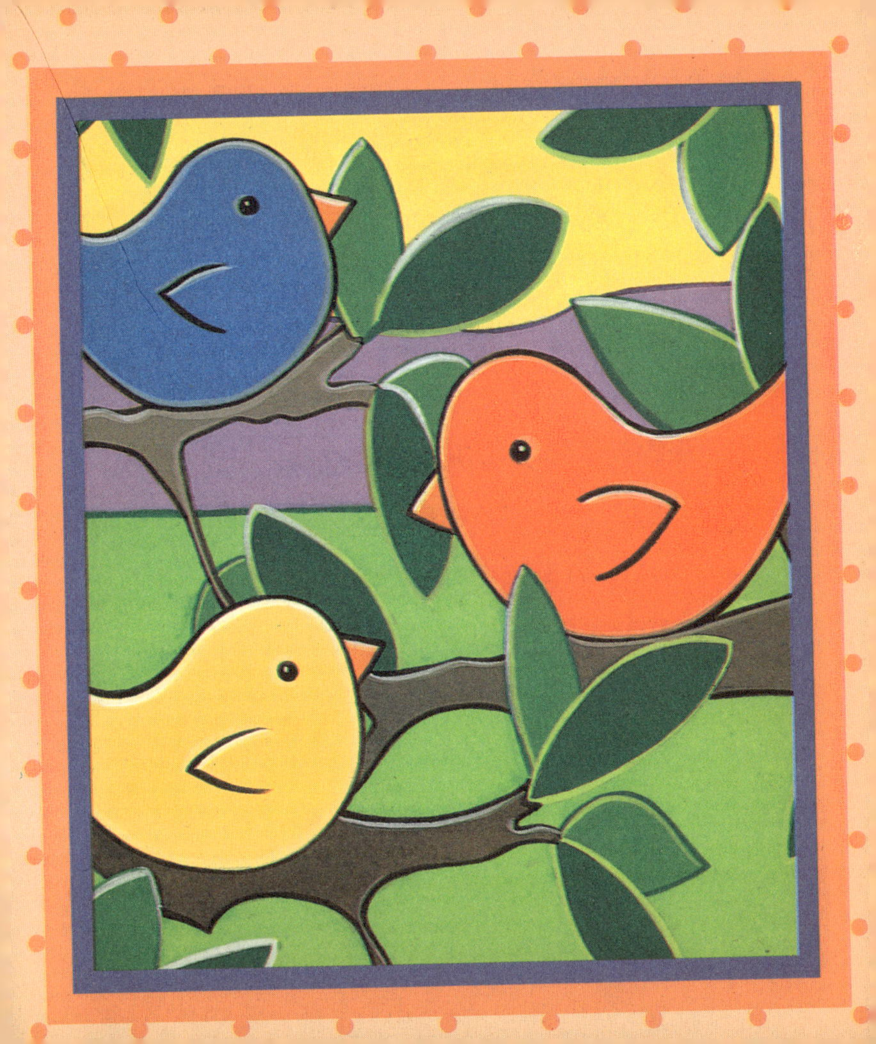

And then God decided
To fill up the seas,
With fishes and dolphins
And whales, if you please.

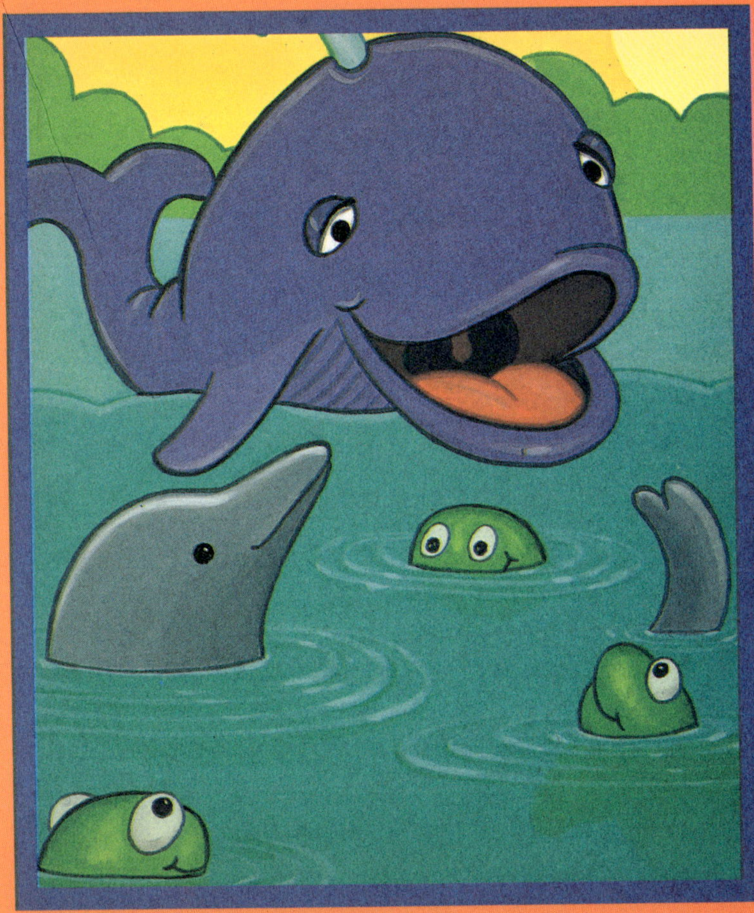

"Well, all that's not bad,"
Said the Lord, *"but there's more."*
So God made a duck
And more beasts than before.

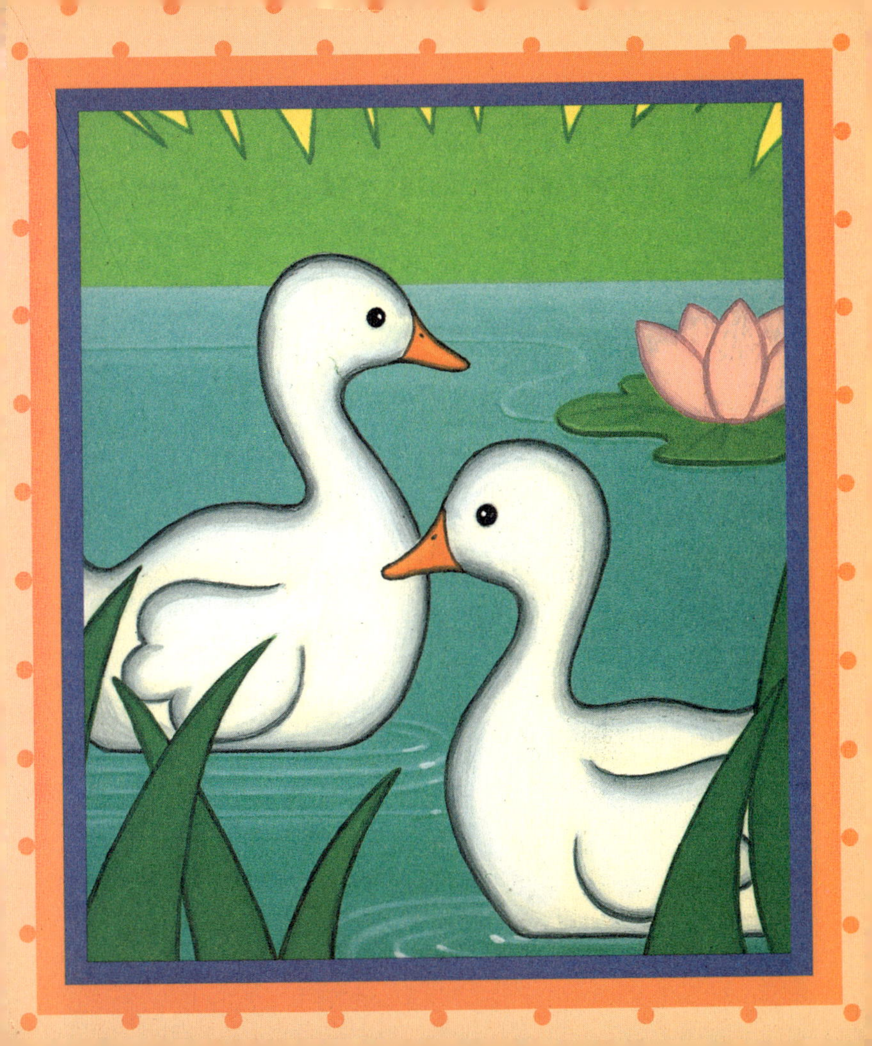

Then on came the camels
And horses and dogs,
The lions, the zebras,
And don't forget frogs.

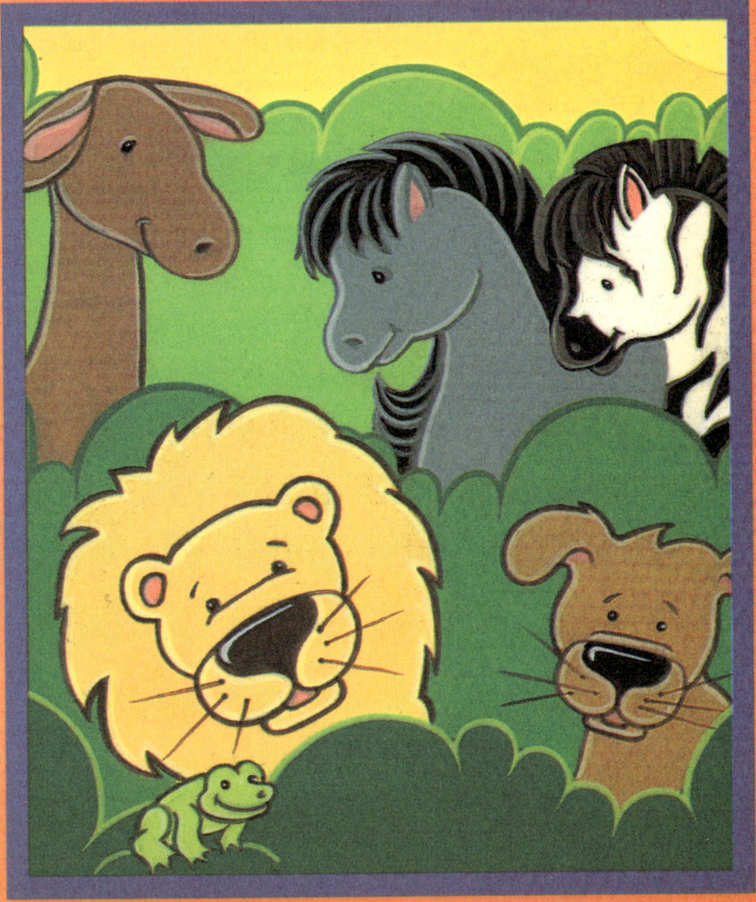

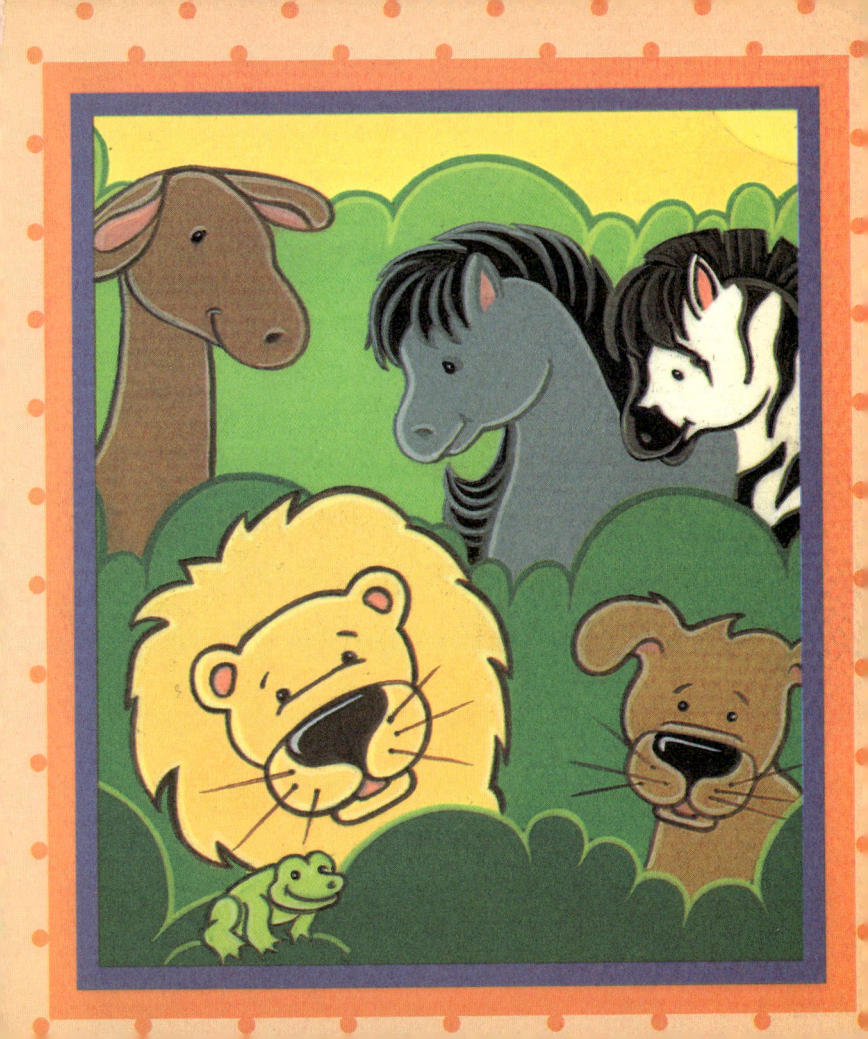

*"But still I'm not done yet.
There's more to my plan."*
And out of the dust
God created a man.

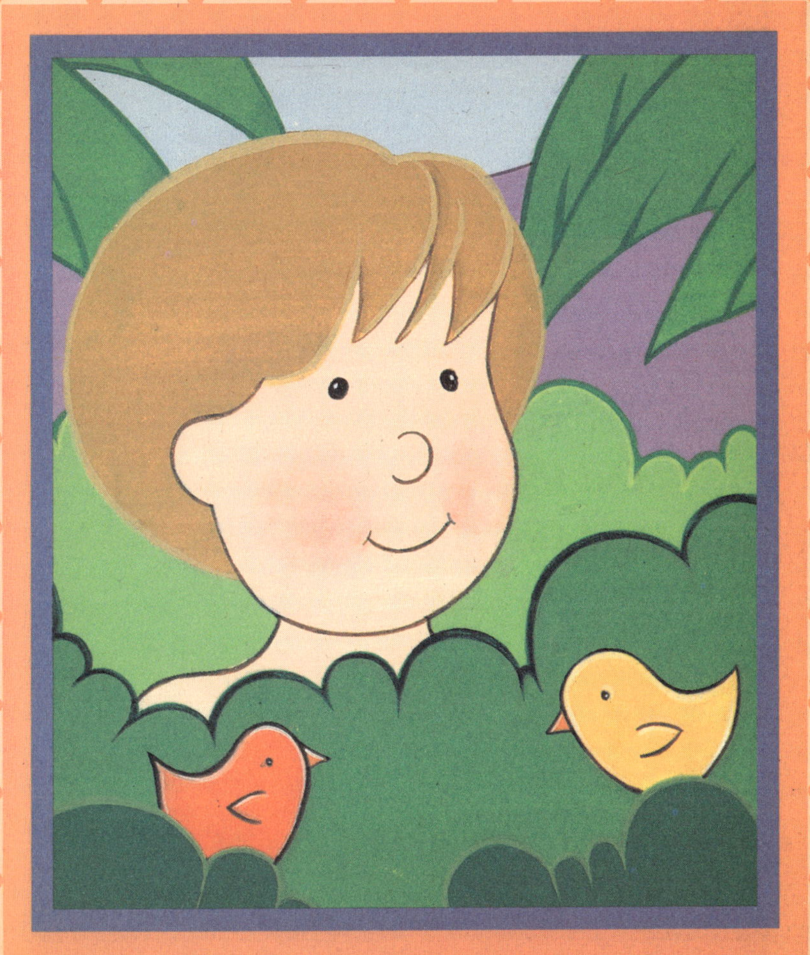

*"I've saved this for last,
And these last are my best."*
And God made a woman.
Then God took a rest.

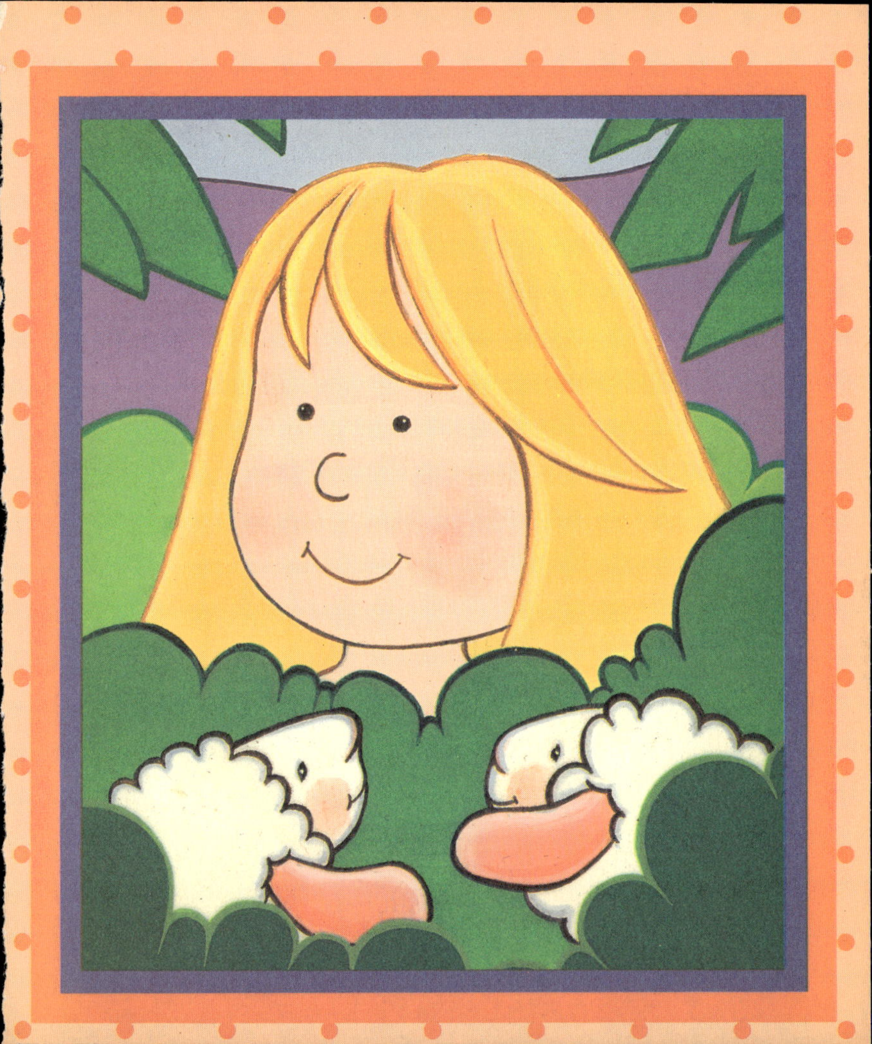

Our God must be great!
Now you know that it's true.
God made all the world,
And He made it for YOU!

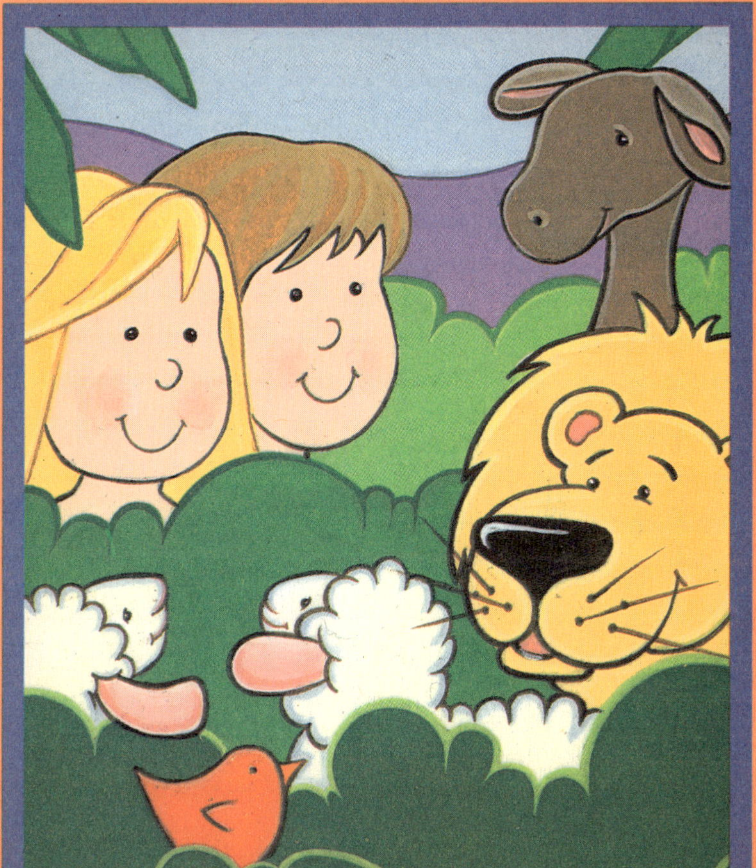

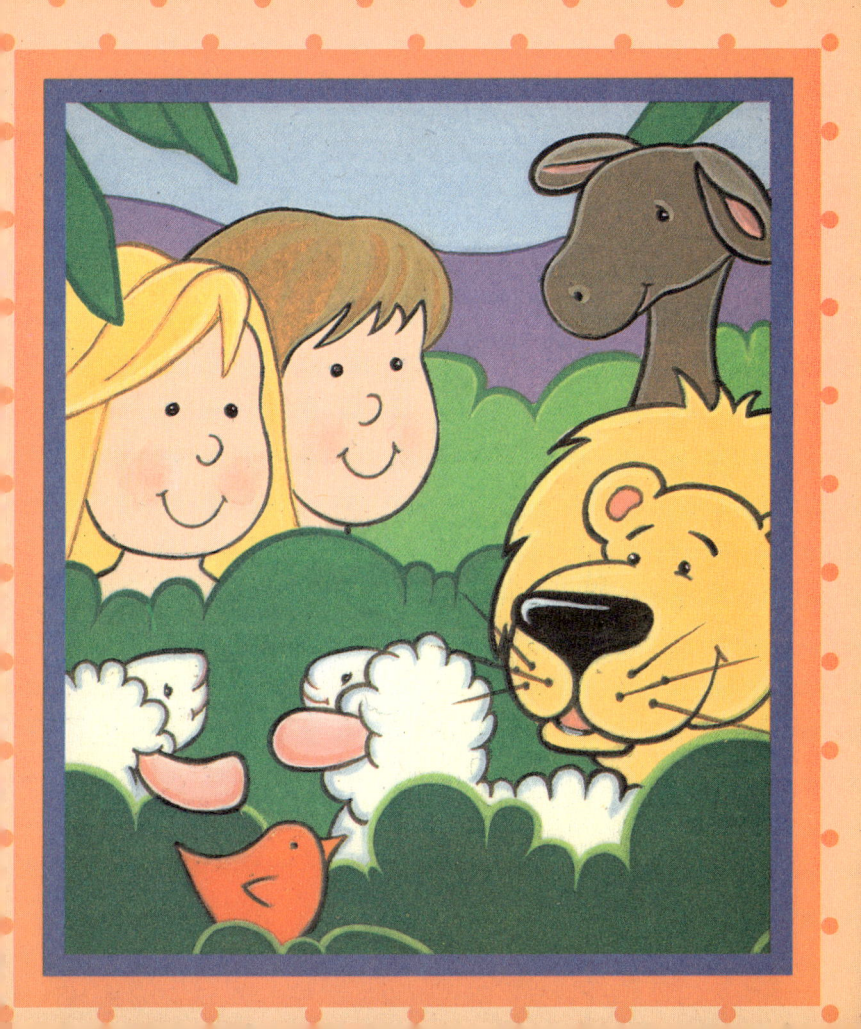

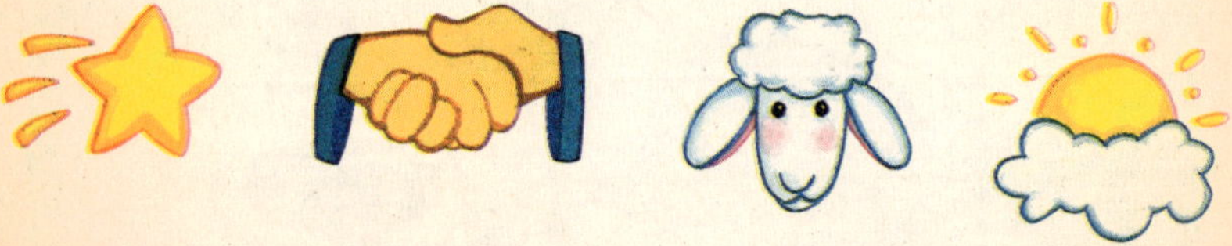